Green Horses on the Walls

poems by

Cristina A. Bejan

Finishing Line Press
Georgetown, Kentucky

Green Horses on the Walls

Dedicated to Alina

ACKNOWLEDGMENTS

All of these poems have appeared on stages across the United States and Romania
performed by Cristina A. Bejan under the stage name 'Lady Godiva':

in Washington DC at Busboys and Poets, Spit Dat, Bloombars and
        Pure Lounge (Pure Poetry led by Orville 'The Poet' Walker)
in Bucharest at Carol 53 alongside Rucsandra Pop
in Raleigh, North Carolina at Noir Lounge (City Soul Café)
in Denver, Colorado at Tattered Cover, Mercury Café, Sacred Voices
        and Creative Strategies for Change Community Cypher

Many of these poems were part of the one-woman show entitled 'Lady Godiva'
(performed by Muslima Musawwir and directed by Star Johnson), which appeared at
Source Theatre as part of the Mead Theatre Lab Program in February 2016.

With special thanks to Jess D. Mekeel for the inspiration and Camelia Crăciun for
editorial help.

COVER DESCRIPTION: This is a photo of (left to right) Bejan's great-uncle Aurelian
Ene and grandparents Marioara and Anghel Bejan strolling through Cişmigiu Park
in Bucharest, Romania circa 1936.

CONTENT WARNING: This book confronts the difficult topics of the crimes of
communism, mental health, and sexual assault.

All views are the author's and names have been changed to protect the privacy of
individuals.

Publisher: Leah Maines
Editor: Christen Kincaid
Cover Art: Cristina A. Bejan
Author Photo: Cristina A. Bejan
Cover Design: Elizabeth Maines McCleavy

Printed in the USA on acid-free paper.
Order online: www.finishinglinepress.com
        also available on amazon.com

Author inquiries and mail orders:
Finishing Line Press
P. O. Box 1626
Georgetown, Kentucky 40324
U. S. A.

Table of Contents

'not for anything important,' said the policeman

Ornate grand facades shelter empty rooms and hallways
The self-corruption of decadence
They take a cigarette break on the balcony
A group of three young women
Too young to know what this building was meant to be
Yet too old to care to make it better
They look out at the throngs of people
The hustle of the city center
The trams
The buses
Throbbing with life
Within and amidst the falling apart, the dying
But that doesn't matter
The DJ mixes beats in the neighboring piazza
In front of the national theatre
After work the three young women will go there
To the rally of one of the many political parties
And dance
And dance
And smoke
And laugh
And hope for a new revolution

Equilibrium

Things could be worse
Parents with cancer
Love of your life leaves you for the priesthood
You could have more than mental health "issues" and actually be totally insane
You could never pause to look at the top of buildings
You could be too self-absorbed to think about your family
You could slip and fall
Be hit by a bus
Forget history
Be annoyed by the symphony of honking cars and barking dogs
Never cry
Not sleep enough
Swear off chocolate

You could blitz through life
You could take those you love for granted
Be cheap and petty
Unforgiving and stupid

But yesterday morning I saw a young city man buy an old country man
    breakfast
And somehow it wasn't charity, it was normal, it was right

People may shit on each other here, but that is not all they do
And when it feels like too much—which it often does
I know I can go home. I know I have a home
And how many people can say that?

I have needed to leave and return so many times
I don't think it will ever stop
All I want now is equilibrium
Vezi? Acum stai în echilibru! [See? Now you are standing in equilibrium!]
Bunicul [the grandfather] said to his granddaughter
As she balanced on a parking pole
Between the Lutheran Church and the Royal Palace

And I walked by on my way to the gym
In a desperate vain attempt to feign a routine
In this Balkan maze of *nebunie* [craziness]
Throw my hands up
Breathe deeply
And tell the stories that were told to me
Someone somewhere, even here, is listening

America World Police, Inside Empty

A US Military base on the banks of the Black Sea
A bus leaves full of men and women in fatigues
Going to the Eastern European capital for a day of museums .... i.e. "Fun"
Headphones blaring hip-hop
After this Sunday
From Mihail Kogălniceanu—MK—being shipped to death
Romania is the gateway to Iraq and Afghanistan
It's death upon death
This same day back home in middle America
News of the soldier's high school best friend
Shot
On the streets of Youngstown

On Efate

On Efate
While doing yoga on our lagoon-side patio
I noticed a canoe in the water
Holding four men who watched me through binoculars
I waved
At that moment my cellphone rang
And the first lady invited me to her island

Beyond language

Escorted to an island that requires an invitation
Another world just on the other side of a resort
So secret that those in the know—know it's there
Those who don't know live in ignorant bliss

An island that transcends language
Because her language itself is secret

There I met the poetess
A distinguished old lady welcomed me into her home
We sat on her veranda
And she giggled when I told her of my admiration

A voice of the revolution she couldn't have been more humble
Why had I been so nervous?

But a secret island is not only giggling grandmothers
Or revolutionary writers
But also a world unseen to so many
A tremendous honor had been bestowed on me

And with that came a fear that arose only after
I ate durian fruit with her niece that afternoon

When the Europeans arrived in the tropical Amazon
Their method of writing was soon observed by the tribal chiefs
To be a tool of power—so those illiterate pretended to be literate
A new form of subordination began

The secret island, these powerful people dominate society already
And now completely unintentionally, thanks to literature and art,

I had been welcomed into a home forbidden to their countrymen

A Tricky Diaspora

I'm from a tricky Diaspora
An assimilate-quick Diaspora
A red lipstick, high heels and skinny perfumed cigarettes Diaspora
The only thing we are known for is not exactly in our history—"Dracula"
  Diaspora
Maybe that's why we say we're from anywhere than we actually are—"Je suis à
  Paris!"
An I can't actually hear the parental accent Diaspora
A my siblings cannot pronounce our family name correctly Diaspora
A too suspicious and yet too trusting Diaspora
A "Shhh, don't talk or they will hear you," Diaspora
A country that you've never heard of Diaspora
An "I silently understand eight languages" Diaspora
A no pressure to get married ever Diaspora
A sex is healthy and beautiful Diaspora
An any race is more beautiful than Caucasian Diaspora
Unless you're a Roma gypsy Diaspora
A politically totally confused Diaspora
A Reagan Realpolitik Diaspora
A "So, you're telling me healthcare isn't free?" Diaspora
All education is always on full scholarship Diaspora
A "What, you don't have at least two graduate degrees?" Diaspora—Dr! Dr!
A knowing the world map Diaspora
A spiritual but not religious Diaspora
A never knowing your grandparents Diaspora
A family history so painful that you just never talk about it Diaspora
A rejoicing through tears when your country's dictator is assassinated
  Diaspora
A real appreciation for a pair of blue jeans Diaspora
A not so ancient history of wearing denim on denim Diaspora
A deep understanding of the origins of rock and roll Diaspora

Ce frumoasă țară e România [What a beautiful country Romania is]

Is it?

Dar în SUA avem un viitor [But in the USA we have a future]

You don't have to be from our Diaspora to have heard that one before.

Nu e rolul meu [It is not my role]

We sat across from each other in this Camden pub
Both blonde
Both 5' 5"
One is a professional model (guess which)
The other a roving intellectual
Last time I saw Mirela was in a photograph
Black and white, she was brunette then and very tiny
Wearing an *ie*—the traditional Romanian blouse
Standing next to *Moş Crăciun*, Galaţi's Santa Claus
"You know, Cris, you were my Neverland."
I-am zis că am ştiut pentru că ea a fost la fel pentru mine [I told her I knew
    because she was the same for me]
"I lived for the next box of toys and clothes
For our grandmother to return from a trip and tell me of you guys
Through photographs, you, Ana and Gabi were my family
I'm not close to my parents you know?
But when *bunica noastră* [our grandmother] died—it all stopped
No more contact from you
And no one ever told me why
I asked my father
Over and over again
And nothing."
"Our fathers are different," I told her.
"My father serious—yours the family rebel."
In that moment I had the chance to tell her …
But she was so happy
And I decided that: *Nu e rolul meu*
It's not my role to tell her that I had been told
Her parents tried to starve our grandmother to death for her apartment
It was 1994
Property had just been returned to Romanians by the state
They locked her in hers
A 90 year old woman with Alzheimer's and deformed hands from a lifetime of
    filling medicine bottles as a pharmacist
My father only found out because a Galaţi friend got wind of the terror
And called him in North Carolina
I was twelve
My sister was ten
My brother was four
And my American grandfather had been dead for two years

I know now that we forgive family
But that doesn't mean that we have to discuss everything
Mirela and I are friends now
Și nu e rolul meu

Under your mattress

Put it under your mattress
The money
The truth
The pain

That's my Romanian father's American mantra.
"Cristina, put this 200 dollars under your mattress.
Cristina, don't tell anyone of the rape, the breakdowns, the sexual harassment.
Just stuff it under your mattress, no one looks there."

I was told early on not to look in our family's secret police file
Which was absurd because I was in that Bucharest archive every day anyway

When I told my friends that I was obeying my father's instructions
Eyebrows raised.
Romanian girlfriends are loyal to family but they also don't take the bullshit
    that American women do.
Cristina, asta înseamnă că trebuie să te uiți. [Cristina, that means that you
    have to look]
I know, I always said.

Under communism there were no banks
There was no wealth
Every man and woman were equal
Equally destroyed
Equally in fear
Equally invisible

But there were ways around the system
As there always are under oppression
Black market ruled
And all the good guys had a prison term as proof of their protest

Don't talk or they'll hear you
So Romania was silent
People listening through the walls
Making love to your wife and everyone knows
It's in your secret police file
I've read those truths

And the risk that they will raid is always there.
Looking for dissidence
Looking for an excuse to torture
Because frankly everyone is just bored under totalitarianism
Not allowed to go anywhere
Not allowed to choose your job
Not allowed to choose your apartment
So you drink, you smoke and you fuck
Reduced to animals.
Ambition is a no-no.
Intelligence the ultimate threat.

So the agents burst in
They've heard you've been keeping a chicken farm illegally on the outskirts
    of Galați
You know, saving money
Defying the system

Bejans protest of course
"N-avem nimic de ascuns." [We have nothing to hide]
"Ba da," Securiștii ["But yes you have," the Secret Police] bark
As they go straight for the bedroom
And flip your mattress.

Opening the Orange Envelope

My veterinarian grandfather was arrested while ice-skating on the open-air rink in Galați in southeastern Romania in 1948 and disappeared to internment in Bucharest. Later my pharmacist grandmother was picked up on her way to the train station in the early 1950s. Both were only guilty of being educated peasants and not members of the Communist Party. Both were tortured and interrogated. And both told their children that nothing had happened but my father knew better than that.

When my father left Romania in 1969 and decided to stay in the USA, he and his family knew what would happen. He became an "Enemy of the State." The harassment began full-force on both sides of the Atlantic. The *Securitate* [The Romanian Secret Police] terrorized my family in Galați and my parents in the States. What does this terror look like? Imagine no conversation being secret. "Don't talk or they'll hear you," was the constant refrain in my grandparents' apartment. Imagine being followed everywhere. Walking down the street. Going to the grocery store. Looking out the window from your home, and someone is standing there in a trench coat smoking, watching you. A secret police officer barging in on you while you are taking a bath and interrogating you in the tub, naked. Worrying that everyone you talk to is an informant, because they probably are. This lasted for my family for twenty years until the Fall of Communism.

My most vivid childhood memories from the 80s are not of listening to JEM or playing with Barbie, but rather they are of my parents routinely sitting us down in the middle of our house in North Carolina and directing us on the assembly line of putting together packages for our relatives in Romania. We prepared them with so much care, stacking the blocks of soap, old T-shirts, coveted blue jeans and cartons and cartons of cigarettes. My father showed us who these packages were going to, with black and white photographs he pulled out of an orange envelope. When he was sleeping or out of the house, I would regularly sneak into his home office upstairs and open the orange envelope and peak into a world forbidden to me.

I just found out from my cousin (the model, who I only knew as a photograph for so long) that our grandfather had built a special bed for himself, above the front door, so that when the *Securitate* would barge in in the middle of the night, they wouldn't see him and arrest him. She also told me that our grandmother, the pharmacist, had self-medicated from her pharmacy for decades trying to control her anxiety induced by this relentless terror. Mirela also introduced me to the concept of inherited trauma, and the studies done on the grandchildren of Holocaust survivors. It all makes sense now: our great-uncle was on the Canal for over a decade, Romania's most notorious labor camp. He returned to his wife (who waited for him) in his village crazy and he died shortly thereafter. Mirela left her promising modeling career in Bucharest to be a psychiatric nurse in London.

And I am a Romanian-American who grew up in comfortable North Carolina. I know that the word "communism" means many things to many people. But this is what it means to me.

About the country I left

Our street gang
Rocks, our block
My brother and I
Grew up defending
The territory
My father had animals
Seeky (*Pisica*) the cat
Castration by boot
And the pigs and chickens
Don't forget the owl
Bad luck
But on the bus back from basketball in the mountains
Nușu stole the stuffed owl
From the lodge where we stayed—
Back to the city and
The great river I grew up on
Fishing and swimming—
Curious floating brown things
And hidden heads in pumpkins
My mother would tell my father
"Shhh, or they will hear you."
Can't talk politics, never
My favorite uncle
Aurelian paid the price.
That country, city, street—
The house of my youth
The room of my birth
That window
That is where—
In there—
I came to be

Green Horses on the Walls

Cai verzi pe pereți [Green horses on the walls]
Asta a fost de la-nceput în mintea mea [That's how it was in the beginning in
    my mind]
Visurile mele [My dreams]
N-au fost posibile [Were not possible]
Am fost nebună [I was crazy]
Bătută în cap [Hit in the head]
Cristina—fii serioasă [Cristina—be serious]
Vrei doar cai verzi pe pereți [You only want green horses on the walls]
Green horses on the walls
The Romanian expression for having delusions
From the start I was told my dreams
Weren't possible
That I was crazy
That I needed to be serious
That theatre was a hobby
I was always merely chasing the green horses
And it was time to grow up
Because they didn't exist
But I know my need to write exists
I know that the open page is the reservoir for my joy and pain
I know the sweat-stained floors of an empty theatre welcome me
I know that my dimensions cannot be confined to a DC-CV
A list of degrees and honors—> now perhaps those don't truly exist
Can they capture a beating heart?
Prayers? Kindness?
Caring for our elders and children?
Or the next play that it is on the tip of my pen and igniting my mind with
    excitement
The straight-jacketed list to DC impress is what confines
And lies
My truth is displayed on the open canvas of my art
My truth runs with the green horses
Through the fields, down Rockville Pike and eventually all the way through
    the heart of DC—14th St.
I hear them calling—
Cristina! *Hai acasă* [Come home]
Calling me home ...
As I walked today through a canopy of trees
I crossed paths with a butterfly

And I came home to write this poem
And neither were or are—delusions.
Cai verzi pe pereți—a durat 34 de ani [Green horses on the walls—it took 34
   years]
Pentru mine să știu [For me to know]
Adânc în inima mea [Deep in my heart]
Că sunt exact cum a creat și a vrut Dumnezeu [That I am exactly how God
   created and wanted]
Și pentru asta sunt pur și simplu mulțumită [And for that I am simply grateful]

Scumpul meu [My dear]

I could kiss you forever
You swept into my life
Totally unexpected
And I can't describe the feelings I have for you
I like you so much it scares me
You listen, ask questions, attempt to understand
And I want to do the same for you
Our first weekend together
Netflix and my cable were out
How convenient!
From now I have to go slow
Take things as they come
No expect
Just enjoy
Please *scumpul meu*
Don't run for the hills
Please let's explore Raleigh
And each other
Holding each other
Hitting snooze
Snuggling
More kissing
Please God
I want all of it.

Înainte [Forward]

As the magnificent sun rose today
I saw God smile
For the first time in years—almost decades
These three months have been beyond magical
You've embraced me with a love and acceptance that is truly superhuman
How did I meet a man of such integrity?
Such honesty?
So genuine?
So loving?
I've fallen in love faster than I could catch myself
And I love you with my entire self, my heart, soul, desire and dreams
Dreams of the future
Mine is yours
We have so much now and ahead
Înainte scumpul meu! [Forward my dear!]
Loving and supportive
Always
#claimed
I will be

Bucharest

It's the little things
Flower shops on every corner
For hello, for goodbye
For welcome, for you're welcome
For *bine ați venit* [welcome]—For it's an absolute pleasure
And for thank you, for I love you
It's gift bags and wrapping paper at every grocery check-out
It's the fumes of gasoline lingering amidst the general smell of pollution
Mixed with cigarettes, mixed with cigars, mixed with, pure, sweet and
    delicious B.O.
All blanketed with the strongest perfume from Paris
It's walking on the street at night
With no fear of harassment or someone revealing a firearm
It's being a woman in all one's femininity and that being OK
It's being a man who loves and hugs and that being OK
It's having coffee with your closest friend and actually having a conversation
It's a world with no agenda
Because all roads lead to nowhere anyway
That's why people escape to where you came from
It's parks full of the elderly spending afternoons watching grandchildren play
It's trams, buses, cars, motorcycles, mopeds, bicycles and the Metro
It's streets that you would rather just walk
Because every piazza leads you to a place you'd like to be
It's a city of theatres, of universities, of libraries,
Of the most infamous nightclubs in Europe
In a language that is secret—because all Romanians speak English fluently
    anyway
It's private, like Eastern Christian Orthodoxy
Where the priests conduct the entire liturgy behind an ornate golden painted
    gate
That private sacred space the packed church of parishioners will never get to
    see
Private like how they—we—don't talk about the past
It's days spent wandering
It's nights spent dreaming
It's a place "where things just happen"
Dynamic, immediate and perpetually young
It's underground brought to light
And it's anyone's—Native, Expat, Diaspora's—playground

#Simplicity

An American girlfriend I met in Bucharest recently told me that the cure to
all my woes would be to:
KEEP IT SIMPLE
Try telling that to the DC girl living the millennial dream of a federal contract
and her own non-profit?
Family duties and issues
Can't go to NC, can't bring myself
Need to make love to a man but DC guys just don't get down like that
I tried again with the perfect candidate with my background, languages and
baggage
He came to me in a dream to tell him to try again
And in real life he texted me that it's not me, it's him (after apologizing for
taking a week to reply because it was the end of the fiscal year at the World
Bank)
I said, "Thanks Alex!"
I learned the simplicity lesson a long time ago
June 10, 2009 I lost a colleague to a brutal racist attack on our Federal building
Hearing his wife's cries at the funeral told me what to do
I gave up a job in Romania and any prospects in the US
To move to an island in the middle of the Pacific
And keep it simple
Just love my man
Do what he needed
Simply be there
Do the groceries, make love, talk to him about his job and anxieties
I was ready
But nothing could prepare me for island life
Everyone knew he had an affair with a tourist before I arrived
"He likes blondes," I said of my brown partner trying to laugh it off.
He pretended we were married everywhere
To the gardener and his pregnant wife
To the Ambassadors of Australia, Kiribati, PNG, New Zealand and their wives
I was owned like women on that island are
But without any of the security
We fought worse in the third world than our second and first world previous
versions of self knew possible
Exile from bedrooms
Visits to work to make up and cry
And one day he raised a hand to me
And I knew it was over

I left under the guise of having a breakdown, which I had had before
I paid both his and my tickets to take me home
And he never paid me back
On the phone he would yell, after I told him my father had been diagnosed
    with cancer, "Port Vila is my city, Cristina! Vanuatu is my country!"
As I'd ask where and when we were supposed to see each other again

It's been simple—eating grapefruit from the front yard
But that's not what my Bucharest friend meant
Simple as someone to talk to
Simple as someone who won't try to use you
Simple as someone who can listen
Simple as someone who will hold you
Simple as someone who won't judge
Simple as someone who isn't entitled
Simple as someone who can love

I told the same friend yesterday that I just need someone to hug
She told me, "Sofia [her daughter] has a pillow.
Grab a pillow."
"Sofia's 11!!!!!!!!!" I shot back.

But maybe Bucharest friend has a point.
She and I can talk endlessly about extramarital affairs
Trans-continental Skype sex
Yet as we—humans—each close our eyes
And hope to open them in the morning
It's just me
Just as I was at prepubescent 11.
Before hormones drove me to lose everything
And tempt me to compromise my empire of 1 right now

Luckily I currently own 4 pillows.
#Simplicity

2010

In our culture of to-do lists
And deadlines

When do we step back and say
It's enough?

I did it. I earned it. It's done.
No more.

When do we answer to ourselves
Instead of other people

After family, comes various institutions—always—
Comes an endless stream of should be, could be, might be, will be

I'm just me. That's all
And I shouldn't have to apologize
Or beg
Or justify

The chatter is endless and unavoidable
Must transcend
And trust

Don't join the rat-race, Cristina, you are not a rat

You weren't then. You are not now.
Breathe.

By doing what you love you have arrived at this point
You always have a choice
Be authentic to yourself
Be cool with that being highly unusual
Savor what you have that is special
You are loved

We each have a proper place on this earth—don't push yourself into something
Trust your inner nature, Tao of Pooh and all that

Follow the birds
When, how and where will I land?

Is it a crime to think that the status quo is pretty darn dull?
It's not that I have always needed to be elsewhere (Life is Elsewhere)—No
It's that I have an insatiable curiosity, a quenchless Wanderlust, an antipathy
   to conformity and zero tolerance for bullshit
At least there is no pole up my ass
But in the meantime
While I am figuring it all out
I desperately need to regain my sense of humor

Raleigh

Fresh on a Wednesday morning
The streets of Raleigh
Just empty
Not of cars, trucks and leaf-blowers—no
Empty sidewalks
Barren of people
A state capital city
With no one walking to work
This should be a city throbbing with life
Instead suburban sprawl has rendered that impossible
Strip-mall paradise
Hipsters with dogs at every brewery
The occasional running pair blitzing past
Inside the coffeshop you find humanity
Who drove here from God knows where
Where are those crisp mornings with energy in the streets?
Where is the park with children playing and grandmothers on benches?
Where is the piazza with lovers holding hands and a fountain flowing?
In this Ayn Randian supreme manifestation of individualism
I feel totally isolated
But I keep reminding myself—this is not Bucharest—this is not DC
Raleigh has its own identity
And I still haven't discovered what it is
One year in and I still don't know
Well I know one thing
I'll keep walking these empty streets
I'll make Raleigh my little Bucharest, my petite DC
Here I go.

My prayer

Immanuel taught me fourteen years ago
Not to pursue things that would not be complete in and of themselves
Never to use something—or someone—in order to get somewhere else—
    obtain something else
The notion of THE end in itself
The stepping stones of life more often than not have you hopping—or me
    hopping—one to the next
Each a means to the next end and then another means to the next end
Ad inf.
There is no more need to hop
No lingering ember of a need to escape
I've somehow landed on the end of itself
And I've now seen that I don't have to pursue or use ever again
My hope and prayer is that I can also be the end in itself
I hope that home can be built
And family created, nurtured and celebrated
That on this pebble in the grand lake of Life
I can continue to knock at your door
Without having to go anywhere
Or forcibly forget anything
Stuff it or suppress it—hold onto the means so I can get to another mirage
    that is never an end.
No more.
No more suffering.
I can cry it all out here in this moment in this place.
And I feel your arms around me—holding me—telling me that it is
    perfectly alright to hurt—to feel—to stand up for myself—finally.
And with your constant whisper in my ear replying to my seeking
I hear you telling me that with the days and the years
Everything that I've seen will make sense
And I will understand why I was given this path
And
With no more hopping, no more escaping, no more means
Breath by breath
Here
I will be free.

The Streets of Johannesburg

Today I wish you were more streets of Johannesburg than boarding school
    and Harvard.
I wish you treated me like the Zulu women you loved then.
Made love to me.
But no you have two phones with emails to send
And a mom to call
Who cannot figure out how the hell to use the Metro at Union Station
And you run to her rescue
The same evening you left me alone—again
As your social life then eclipsed whatever embers of our romance were left
"Cristina, I want to stay out after 9pm."
"Cristina, I want to watch TV with commercials."
"Cristina, I need you to be there when the potential tenants come to see I
    have a white girlfriend."
"Cristina, no other man would put up with your illness."
And I did what you wanted. I believed you.
My self-esteem vanished with my free will
And I was just an extension of you, another arm of the proverbial
    African family octopus—there was no ME anymore. I was empty.
"But you've grown the most important way this year, Cristina, spiritually."
And that is the only thing that you, Nathaniel, said to me that was in fact true.
And my God protected me from a hellish future that would have seen me a
    slave
You would have owned me. I would have been simply property.
And a vehicle to bear your children. A vehicle to cook your meals. To clean
    your goddamn bathroom for Christ's sake. Yes, I just wrote that down and
    said it. (Hey, nothing is off-limits on the open mic.)
That's it.
For many women there is safety in that. So I don't judge others.
But this isn't the Comoros Islands.
You were drawn to me by all the things you ended up despising
My degrees, my intellect, my plays, my poems
My hippie den in the artist commune in Petworth
Where you found a freedom you could not in your basement sleeping next to
    your brother, in a cramped shared space with your mom sleeping in the
    back bedroom.
In my bed you told me of your drug addicted father
You told me of your childhood friend's death
You told me of being a teenager in Moroni, listening to the Lauryn Hill album
    on repeat when it first came out

But there were certainly red flags

You were shocked when it was our third date and you asked me to go down
    on you and I said No.

"That would mean I go down on everyone, I said."

You didn't get it.

You invited me to Peru on my own dime and I tried to explain to you that I
    don't have the money that you are used to DC women having.

You about blew up on the bench in front of the World Bank.

I tried to calm you down.

I went. I paid for my trip!

And I climbed Manchu Picchu hell yeah I did.

Or a month later when you picked me up from the Sculpture Garden ice rink

Only to lecture me endlessly on how I don't dress up enough for you

How you feel disrespected

I tried to explain that I am from North Carolina

And I naturally have an afro

But it made no difference.

So I could've walked away

But your charisma and false promises prevailed

And one sweet nothing about commitment and the future at a time

Well, I fell for it—fell for you

You told me you loved me

And I did love you back

I loved the hell out of you

You have NEVER been loved the way I loved you

And I know that for sure

And I know that you don't care one bit

Online dating is like shopping

The bananas went bad so you dropped them out back in the trash

Rotting, stinking, bruised

And yet isn't that when they're the most delicious?

Not to you.

You need the pristine, untarnished

Ivy-League, Six-Figure, Fluent-in-Real-Estate DC Chick

(Funny how Real Estate is the only language I didn't immediately pick up.)

You know that chick who doesn't know that she can create her own orgasm.

That chick who desperately needs a boyfriend.

That chick who will worship you.

Who will brag about your triumph in bureaucracy on the 4th Floor of the
    Banque Mondiale.

A chick who won't let herself realize how spoiled, pampered and sad you are
Still glued to your mother's teet.
Willful ignorance is ugly as fuck no matter the situation.
And your own ignorance frankly shameful.
You may own the Bible but being the only book you own ….
How can you tell me Harvard is better than Oxford?
One book—no matter the book—should itself be a crime.

Lasantha

You are darker than any man I have ever known
But the light inside you more blinding than the sun

When we met the world cracked and everything I thought was right just
  flipped
Some people think you are guilty of war crimes
Others know you are a general serving your country
You are a husband, a father, and the caretaker of so many in your traditional
  family

Between embassies, parties, the Kennedy Center and me forcing you to watch
  ice hockey
You became my best friend.
But it was only when I told you of my darkest wound
That love overtook me like a demon

"Oh, the agonies you have known."
That's what you said.
And with that being the first human being who did not recoil from my
  personal horror.
You listened and told me to be cool, it's all in the past.
I don't need to be haunted by it all any more.

So I shed my clothes like I did ten years of defenses.

You are not my boyfriend

"You are not my boyfriend," I told the Sri Lankan Defense Attaché last week
He countered with a bizarre psychoanalysis of the difference between South
    Asian and Western women
Apparently South Asian women are controlling yet dependent
Whereas Western women are not controlling and independent
Says the man who has two live-in Sri Lankan women to cook for him and
    iron his three piece suits
And one of them spoke up to him recently
He told me that's what he hates most: women who act like men.

I bit my tongue, with my American upbringing, my European background
    and my DC career.
Funny how Lasantha has never thought that I act like a man over the past
    eight months

This past Saturday I spent the day with my former professor, an eminent
    philosopher from Senegal
We shared a long lunch in French and ran on Africa time,
As I got to know his wife, his daughter and his most important disciple who
    was visiting New York from Paris with her husband and two year-old son
After our dessert of fruit and Senegalese tea,
Malik showed me some photo albums of his family when they were still in
    Dakar
These photos were all in their home:
Gorgeous photos of his wife,
baby photos,
photos from family dinner,
photos of friends coming over,
photos of dance parties,
photos of Malik in his glasses at his desk, with one of his sons on his knee

I cried on the bus back to DC

Moral Force of Character?

You say I have no right to believe in morality?
That there is no universal good and evil?
This is my answer
The reason I know is that I've already been to Hell
More than once
The first time was being pushed down a road while I was too drunk to walk
    the other way
And I kept saying, "But I want to go to St. Antony's."
After showing me photos of skeletons on your computer from your doctoral
    research
You fucked me on a bed that had not yet crossed my mind
I woke up smelling death
Then I had to live a label that I knew also represented the worst of humanity
But listen I am the only one with a passport from my father's country that is
    a member of this elite label
Could I ever talk to him, or Romania, about the fact that the label is a LIE?
So I hid it, from everyone, for ten years.
In and out of spaces that that label never goes
One example?
The dungeon that is Duke University Hospital Psychiatric Emergency Room
I thought I had already seen Hell in Oxford
No.
I was there again, for the second time
In a room with lounge chairs facing each other
And two rooms for solitary confinement in the corners
A heroin addict from the mountains coming off it and going hysterical
A Korean War vet with more dignity than any fucking label, and he's
    homeless
A young student who had been accused of being crazy by his university and
    the Durham police when he saw and called out HATE
A woman with no teeth who could eat jello but not speak
A man who belonged to a gang for brown people, with that acronym
    tattooed to his forehead
Another woman who resembled more a wild animal than a human being in
    speech and behavior
And finally my friend who I cannot name because I fear for her safety
Who was brought in with force as she screamed in Arabic
The nurses and doctors were at a loss

They couldn't communicate with her
I asked the nurse, "Where's she from?"
Answer: Morocco
I approached the shaking lady in French
Bonsoir madame [Good evening madame]
Qu'est-ce qui vous est arrivé [What has happened to you?]
Je n'ai aucun lien avec cet hôpital [I don't have any connection to this
    hospital]
Qu'est-ce qui s'est passé? [What has happened?]
Only to discover that her husband was beating her up
And told the police that she was the homicidal one
After talking as a group for days and an evening of eating pizza watching
    Duke basketball
A new man came to this town
He said nothing
He just watched
And the last thing I remember from Hell Round-Two
Is this person looking me in the eye
And telling me
That I had it all figured out.

To my rapist—or 'the man who raped me' rather
—with Gratitude

Thank you for ruining the word "my"

Thank you robbing me of my innocence

Thank you for making sex about penetration rather than about love

Thank you for the nightmares that regularly occur at 5 am starring a man I
  don't know having sex with me and then me worried until I wake up that
  I have AIDS

Thank you for making me—like so many other victims—too scared and
  ashamed to report what you had done

Thank you for proving that all you have to be is a white man of privilege to
  get away with a crime

Thank you for proving once again that all you have to be is a white man of
  privilege, a Rhodes Scholar and a sexual predator to succeed in
  Washington

Thank you for never knowing the terror you have introduced me to

Thank you for preventing me from ever speaking to pre-2005 "me" again—
  that's by far the most painful friendship I have ever lost

Thank you for stealing the small part of me that was able to love me—since
  your victorious date-rape I've only known self-hatred

Thank you for being responsible for the fact that I am broke would you
  consider paying my medical bills?

Thank you for reminding me that money doesn't mean contentment but I
  use the word *remind* because I already knew that before we met

Thank you for introducing me to HALDOL—the psychiatric drug that
  erased my handwriting for two years—it literally removed my ability to
  hold a pen. How's that for the writer?

Thank you for giving me a chance to encounter Evil

For now I know exactly what this battle is about

Thank you for being oblivious to the horror that you are responsible for

Thank you for hurting not just me, but by proxy every person that I love

Your poison has spread like a virus through my damaged self

Thank you for proving that not all rape victims look alike

Thank you for proving that there is a reason for the "little black dress"
  stereotype as I was indeed wearing one

Thank you for not doing what I asked you to do

Thank you for not listening

For not honoring what your date—the first date—requested

Thank you for proving that "consent" is a murky concept

And that at the end of the day if the perpetrator wants it, he can just take it

Because then he's a stud

And I'm a slut

Because that's what everyone's told
And what everyone believes
Thank you for proving it all true
Everything you hear as a woman growing up
Thank you for my experiencing slut-shaming—I knew what that word
    meant long before I ever heard it
Thank you for the no hope in myself, thank you for the destructive
    decisions, thank you for the survival, thank you for the need to stay
    stable—just stable—but never happy
Because ten years ago the word "happiness" was erased from my vocabulary
As you used the word to justify your pathetic need to get laid
Thank you for making me settle to live in the steady state called "Sad."
Thank you for a fear of the Metro that pre-dated the Paris attacks as any
    commuting day I could see you
Thank you for preventing me from having goals for my life
Thank you for throwing a quiet Catholic girl into unbelief and suspicion
Thank you for making my spiritual world confused, turning a calm sky into
    a cyclone
And thank you for the invasion of Hate in my heart, soul, mind and self
Hate was only an abstract concept until I met you
Thank you for being the reason I couldn't return to the States, I hopped from
    country to country running away from you—I got to see the world
Thank you for forcing me to speak Romanian—my language of heritage and
    spirit but as I've said here—I'm of the Diaspora—and the best thing
    Romanians do is assimilate
It's thanks to you that I have another language as sanctuary that my spirit—
    that I can retreat to when I remember the last thing you said to me, so
    plainly though I was so wasted that night: " I want to fuck you." In
    English.
Thank you for being a very clear enemy
And thank you for being such a worthless human being
That I can call you meaningless today
You who have literally shaped the trajectory of my life and determined the
    state of my ill-health until now
Not anymore
Thank you for being so unimportant and such a bad tyrant
That I can break my own shackles
It only took me ten years
But this is how it goes for victims

People can tell you: forgive, move on, it's in the past
But every day the victim has so much to thank the rapist for
See?
So, my rapist, thank you for your exit today from my mind and life
For from here on out you shall exist only in my art
As my creativity was always the one thing you could not touch
And I will always thank God for that.

Despre țara din care venim —Ana Blandiana (b. 1942)

Hai să vorbim
Despre țara din care venim.
Eu vin din vară,
E o patrie fragilă
Pe care orice frunză,
Căzând, o poate stinge,
Dar cerul e atât de greu de stele
C-atârnă uneori pân' la pământ
Și dacă te apropii-auzi cum iarba
Gâdilă stelele râzând,
Și florile-s atât de multe
Că te dor
Orbitele uscate ca de soare,
Și sori rotunzi atârnă
Din fiecare pom;
De unde vin eu
Nu lipsește decât moartea,
E-atâta fericire
C-aproape că ți-e somn.

About the country from which we come
—translated by Cristina A. Bejan

Let's talk
About the country from which we come.
I come from summer,
It is a fragile native land
That any falling leaf,
Can extinguish,
But the sky is so heavy with stars
Sometimes it hangs to the ground.
And if you get close – you hear how the grass
Tickles the laughing stars
And there are so many flowers
That your eyes sting
Scorched as if by the sun,
And round suns hang
From every tree;
From where I come
Only death is missing,
There is so much happiness
That you almost fall asleep.

Ultima suflare —Nina Cassian (1924 – 2014)

Îmi cad literele din cuvinte
cum mi-ar cădea dinții din gură.
Bâlbâială? Sâsâială?
Sau e mutenia de pe urmă?

Îndură-te, Doamne,
de cerul gurii mele,
de omușorul meu,
acest clitoris din gâtlejul meu,
vibratil, sensibil, pulsatoriu,
explodând
în orgasmul limbii române.

**The last breath
—translated by Cristina A. Bejan**

For me letters are falling out of words
just as if my teeth were falling out of my mouth.
Am I stammering? Is it a lisp?
Or is dumbness—complete silence—at last?

Have mercy, Lord,
for the roof of my mouth,
for my uvula,
this clitoris in my throat,
vibrating, delicate, throbbing
exploding
into the orgasm that is Romanian.

CPSIA information can be obtained
at www.ICGtesting.com
Printed in the USA
LVHW031139090720
660201LV00004B/105